Who Cares

Matt Woodhead

methuen | drama

LONDON · NEW YORK · OXFORD · NEW DELHI · SYDNEY

METHUEN DRAMA
Bloomsbury Publishing Plc
50 Bedford Square, London, WC1B 3DP, UK
1385 Broadway, New York, NY 10018, USA
29 Earlsfort Terrace, Dublin 2, Ireland

BLOOMSBURY, METHUEN DRAMA and the Methuen Drama logo are
trademarks of Bloomsbury Publishing Plc

First published in Great Britain by Oberon Books 2017
This edition published by Methuen Drama 2021

A catalogue record for this book is available from the British Library.

A catalog record for this book is available from the Library of Congress.

ISBN: PB: 978-1-3503-0683-7
ePDF: 978-1-3503-0684-4
eBook: 978-1-3503-0685-1

Series: Modern Plays

Gaddum
...

LUNG

THE LOWRY

LUNG and The Lowry in partnership with Gaddum
present

Who Cares
by Matt Woodhead

curious
minds

THE
LECHE
TRUST

Gaddum
...

Salford City Council

Supported using public funding by
**ARTS COUNCIL
ENGLAND**

CAST

Connor	Luke Grant
Nicole	Lizzie Mounter
Jade	Liyah Summers

CREATIVE & PRODUCTION TEAM

Engagement Officer	Madiha Ansari
Production Manager	Andreas Ayling
Technical Stage Manager	Tom Booth
Engagement Manager and Associate Director	Gitika Buttoo
Fundraiser	Joshua Chua
Producer	Ellie Claughton
Sound Designer	Owen Crouch
Company Stage Manager	Tracey-Anne Cutbush
Assistant Producer	Camille Koosyial
Assistant Director	Qasim Mahmood
Designer	Jen McGinley
Dramaturg	Helen Monks
Lighting Designer	Will Monks
Vocal Coach	Gary Owston
Director and Writer	Matt Woodhead

Acknowledgements

Jo Aldridge, Sir Rod Aldridge OBE, FRSA, Nigel Banks, Battersea Arts Centre, Hannah Bristow, Gitika Buttoo, George Caple, Eileen Cunnah, Grace Dickson, Erin Doherty, Christine Edzard and the team at Sands Film Studio, Jeremy Glover CBE, Camilla Gordon, David Graham, Grace Gummer, HighTide Theatre, Chris Hill, Clive Holland, Joe Holders, Suzy Humphries, Inga Hirst, Kelly Hurst, Barbara Keeley MP, Emma Lambert, George Leigh, Verity Leigh and the team at Summerhall, Looping the Loop Festival, Sarah McDonald-Hughes, Adam McGuigan, Andy McNamee, Charlie Moore, Richard Norton-Taylor, David Palmer, Daniel Phelps, Joey Phillips, Katie Potter, Deborah Rees, Luke W. Robson, Gilly Roche, Stacey Sandford, Tamar Saphra, Sell A Door Worldwide, Helen Sheard, Caitriona Shoobridge, George Spender, Olivier Stockman, Sam Steiner, David Stewart, Lisa Stone, Jessica Temple, Ralph Thompson, Chris Thorpe, Dan Todd, Cat Tyre, Hannah Tyrrell-Pinder, Gemma Wilson, Konstantinos Vasdekis and the team at Oberon.

Thank you to all of the staff and young people at Onside Youth Zones and all of the staff and young people at Aldridge Education. Julia Fawcett OBE and The Lowry, especially Lee Brennan, Steve Cowton, Matthew Eames, Adam Kent, Emma Lambert, Rhiannon McKay-Smith, Charlie Moore, Jennifer Riding, David Stuart and Claire Symonds. A huge thank you to Dave Clare for your endless amount of support and help in bringing this show to life. Special thanks to Lynsey O'Sullivan from The Lowry, without whose original vision and ongoing support and leadership this project could not have happened. All of the staff and young people at Gaddum and its Salford Carers Service, including Charlotte Brown, Sam Palmer and especially Paul Moran for his unwavering support and commitment.

A special thank you to Antonia-Rae, Ciaron, Kerry and Paige and their families who bravely shared their stories with us.

PRODUCER – LUNG

Founded in Barnsley in 2012, LUNG is a campaign led verbatim theatre company that tours work nationally. We work closely with different communities to make verbatim theatre and hidden voices heard. LUNG creates work that shines a light on political, social and economic issues in modern Britain, using people's actual words to tell their stories.

'Piercing, Relevant, Terrifying And Beautifully Told'
★★★★★
WhatsonStage on *Trojan Horse*

'Infectious'
★★★★
London Evening Standard on *E15*

'Powerful And Devastating'
★★★★
The Guardian on *Chilcot*

'A Company To Watch'
★★★★
The Stage on *The 56*

LUNG's most recent productions include: *The 56*, *E15*, *Chilcot*, *Who Cares* and *Trojan Horse*.

www.lungtheatre.co.uk

PRODUCER – THE LOWRY

The Lowry is a world class arts centre based in Salford, committed to using the arts to enrich people's lives. The Lowry works closely with artistic partners to offer a diverse programme of theatre, opera, musicals, dance, music, comedy, digital and visual art.

At the heart of our work is a belief in the power of the arts as a tool for social change and a commitment to young people in the local community.

As a registered charity with strong local partnerships these projects enable the most 'At Risk' young people to have access to life changing opportunities; to learn new skills, improve their wellbeing and to have a voice through the art that they make.

This exciting work brings together high quality artists with young people who are experiencing challenges in their life. Through this interaction young people explore their own self-expression, political thought and creative ideas, making work which challenges the world to stop and listen.

www.thelowry.com

GADDUM

Salford Carers Service is part of Gaddum. At Gaddum, we treat everyone as individuals. We really get to know those we help, understanding their world to offer a range of support that's right for them. Our promise of tailored support is made possible by our breadth and depth of knowledge, through our unwavering commitment to the local people of Greater Manchester.

Gaddum Carers Service listen to what support is needed by young carers, deliver that support where possible and lobby for change across Greater Manchester where necessary in order to help carers voices be heard. We have worked in Salford for nearly 20 years.

We work with young carers to build their confidence in and resilience to their caring roles including emotional and practical support. We also provide a safe space to talk, express themselves and have respite from their caring responsibilities.

For information on our service, please visit www.gaddum.org.uk

This is our story but there are many more.
There are 700,000 young carers in the UK and loads who remain
unidentified. If you're a young carer, don't stay hidden.
Talk to someone. You don't have to do it alone.

Antonia-Rae, Ciaron, Kerry, Paige

Foreword

Young carers are children and young people, 17 and under, who provide unpaid care to a family member because of a disability, illness, mental health condition, or a drug or alcohol dependency.

Common tasks for a young carer may include practical tasks (e.g. cooking, housework, shopping, managing the family budget and collecting prescriptions) and personal care (e.g. bathing, toileting dressing, helping with mobility). Some are also required to give emotional support to a parent experiencing mental health and / or drug and alcohol problems.

It is estimated that there are more than 700,000 young carers in the UK. They are often hidden, isolated and unidentified; a hidden army caring without support.

The Lowry is a large scale arts centre where we present the best of local, national and international art through a varied programme of dance, drama, theatre, circus, digital and visual arts. Above all else, The Lowry is deeply rooted in Salford, an area of significant deprivation where we aims to use the arts as a vehicle for social change.

In 2011 I picked up the phone to Paul at Salford Young Carers Service for the first time, asking if he would like to work together on a new project that would give young carers a voice through creativity and the arts. His response was sceptical.

'A creative project? With young carers? Doing what, exactly?'

But luckily, despite his hesitation, he met me anyway and that was the start of our six year partnership.

Salford Young Carers Service is part of The Gaddum Centre, Manchester's oldest social welfare charity. It supports carers aged 17 and under to achieve their full potential while allowing them to explore and address the issues they face as carers.

Over the past six years working together we have had many challenges, successes and had lots of learning. But one thing we know for sure, because we have seen it, experienced it and lived it first hand, is that the arts are special in the way that they can allow children and young people to be seen, to be heard and to make change.

Across England there are great differences in the quality, reach and strength of local young carer's services. Depending on where you live, the support available to you could be limited. The result is hundreds of thousands of young carers left to deliver high levels of care in silence, alone and without support.

In 2016, The Lowry then commissioned a new production in partnership with Salford Young Carers Service, which would be made through a large scale creative project with young carers in Salford. The concept being that we would make a high quality verbatim production that would give an honest and truthful platform for young carers in Salford.

The Lowry approached LUNG as verbatim specialists to meet the young people and to explore what it would mean to follow and interview a group of young carers in Salford for nearly two years. They began to build up a picture of their day to day lives, and to craft that into a professional production.

Who Cares highlights the reality facing some young people who – often under the radar of professionals, their schoolteachers and friends – provide care to family members with a physical disability, an illness, a mental health issue or a drug or alcohol dependency. Most importantly it gives a voice to real young carers in Salford who, through the play, can speak directly to audiences.

At the start of this project the young people told us that they wanted to open their front door and allow us access to their world because they wanted to speak on behalf of other young carers up and down the country who don't have a voice.

We are so proud of how brave, tenacious and strong these young people are to share their stories with you, so that we can, through this play, allow other hidden young carers to be seen. *Who Cares* is a celebration of these amazing young people who inspire us constantly with their humour, resilience and passion.

Lynsey O'Sullivan *(Director of Learning & Engagement at The Lowry)* and **Paul Moran** *(Young Carers Manager at Salford Young Carers Service)*

Who Cares

Characters

Connor – 15

Jade – 18

Nicole – 13

Setting

The majority of the action of the play takes place at a school in Salford. Flashbacks occur in different years for each carer. Bubble sections are set in the place the original interview took place.

Performance Notes

Who Cares uses a variety of different story telling techniques, most prominently direct address and re-enactment.

/ towards the end of a line indicates when the next character should start speaking.

6.45am.

An alarm rings.

CONNOR   At quarter to seven the alarm rings.
          I take a breath, then it starts. Mum has
          tea and toast in bed while I make her
          appointments, put my uniform on
          and / I pack my bag.

JADE   I pack my bag and triple check I've got
          my coursework. I look at the clock and
          decide to skip / breakfast.

NICOLE   Breakfast this morning is last night's
          takeaway. I eat it while blasting out
          Twenty One Pilots. I load the washing
          machine, do the dishes and turn on the
          shower. The water isn't even hot before
          Mum is banging on the door being like
          'You should have left five minutes ago.'
          Shit, / I'm gonna be late.'

ALL   I'm gonna be late.

JADE   Growing up with a deaf brother is all
          I've ever known. When I was taught
          to speak, I was taught to sign. Even
          though Will is four years older, I grew up
          looking out for him.

          We've always been a normal family
          though. Mum worked as a social worker
          and Dad was a heavy goods driver.
          I remember when I was little, Dad would
          sneak into my room and whisper 'How
          do you fancy a day off school?' We'd
          always be scared of waking Mum, so I'd
          get dressed dead quick and sneak out

the front door. In his truck we'd go all over. Brighton, London, even Belgium. You name it we drove there. He had this blue fleece which smelt of petrol and cheap aftershave. It was absolutely rancid and I'd never take it off. Until I was eight that was my life. Driving with my Dad.

CONNOR	In half an hour I'm up, ready and out the house. I check I've got my keys.
ALL	Bus pass
NICOLE	Chewing gum
ALL	Planner
JADE	Hand sanitizer
ALL	Phone
CONNOR	Nintendo 3DS
ALL	Headphones
CONNOR	Even if I'm late, I stop before I lock the door. I need a moment to think because I don't know what will be waiting for me when I come home.
NICOLE	When I was two, Dad left. I remember it happened in the middle of the night because I was in my pyjamas. I got out of bed, ran straight downstairs and Mum spent the next hour telling me everything was gonna be alright. I used to think Mum and Dad might get back together. But now I'm too old to believe in fairy tales.
JADE	I sign to Will *(she signs)* 'Tea will be later tonight and it's shepherd's pie.' Before he can complain / I'm out the door.

NICOLE	I'm out the door and I don't look back. I can't deal with another late mark. All teachers keep saying is 'Year 9 is an important time. You mustn't let standards slip.' It's frustrating because they don't realise / there's a proper reason I'm late.
ALL	There's a proper reason I'm late.
CONNOR	Ever since she was young Mum looked after her family. Her sister was born without a fully developed heart and then her parents got ill. But it didn't get in Mum's way. When she got older she got a high-powered job, raised me and kept on caring.
	It's strange to think about that now. But why look back? It won't change anything, you can't stop it from happening. Time is short, I'll reminisce when I'm older. Can we talk about something else? I dunno, anything. Ask me about school.

2

7.55am.

NICOLE	My best mate Brandon is waiting outside. We dump his bike in the back garden and start the journey in. / Mondays are the worst.
CONNOR	Mondays are the worst now I'm in year 11. It's maths, English, physics, RE, computer science, German and double geography. I turn the corner of my road, run past the old library and see / the number 36.

ALL	The number 36 is packed, there aren't any seats.
JADE	And when year 13 strut on, you can literally taste the air. It's usually a mix between Lynx Chocolate and Britney Spears Radiance. When they come onto the top deck I take one last gasp, hold my breath and brace myself for / the journey in.
NICOLE	The journey into school just goes on and on. It would actually be quicker to walk. I notice Connor on his own at the front of the bus. I think about saying hi but me and Brandon are making a snowstorm with pages of the Metro. I add it to my Snapchat Story. In the end we're crammed on that bus / for over forty-five minutes.
CONNOR	For over forty-five minutes my nose is pushed into the arm pit of a year 12. It's hot, sweaty and difficult to breathe. This bus might have WI-FI, but I've already caught every Pokémon on Pokémon Mystery Dungeon. Eventually the doors open and / everyone piles off.
ALL	Everyone piles off.
JADE	I sprint over the road and I'm just about to make it through the gates when I get a Facetime from Will. I ask *(she signs)* 'Are you okay?' I haven't got time to chat but he's confused about his new medication.
	When I finally arrive at registration, my form tutor pulls me up in front of the entire class. I've told him what's going

on at home, but he doesn't get it. He's like 'Jade, you're always late, what's your excuse this time?' Everyone stares as I get tongue tied. I go boiling hot and try to explain but the words won't come out. It feels like the whole classroom is going to swallow me up.

<u>3</u>

8.45am.

NICOLE   At registration it's all kicking off. Basically, Erica accused Chantelle of stealing her pen. Chantelle insists she didn't so things have hit breaking point. Form is in a science lab, so we're on these really tall stools and Erica is being like, 'If you keep my pen I'm gonna snatch your weave.'

CONNOR   Today we have a supply teacher whose eyes bulge out. If you're caught with your phone it's a Friday detention, but I've found a way to link my phone to my smart watch. I message Mum on the sly. I text her while he reads the register.

NICOLE   By now the drama has escalated. It's clear that Chantelle has attached her extensions to her roots, so Erica is actually dragging her off the stool by her scalp. Then there's this weird pause and Erica stands up, holding a clump of Chantelle's hair like a trophy.

JADE   Assembly is always first thing for year 13, so while the teachers go into the hall, I hide in the toilets.

NICOLE	The truth is, I stole Erica's pen. And I'd do it again.
JADE	Mr O'Sullivan has started doing these cringe assemblies where he talks about the future and I'm just like 'No thanks, I can't think about that right now.' I go into one of the cubicles, Facetime Will and ask *(she signs)* 'Have you managed to take your medication okay?' Then I just sit and wait for assembly to end.
NICOLE	A teacher comes in and sends Erica to the head. While everyone watches Chantelle fish her weave out the bin, I put my phone in my blazer pocket and wire my earphones through my sleeve so I'm ready for maths.
	At school if you're caught doing anything wrong you get a behaviour point. We're only three weeks into term and I've already got twenty-five. I listen to music in lessons, it takes my mind off things. It makes me feel like I'm somewhere else.
JADE	Teachers are always on patrol for sixth formers who skive assembly, but they never check the third floor toilets. I take a minute to breathe and then / the bell goes and it's period 1.
ALL	The bell goes and it's period 1.
NICOLE	1,400 kids pour into the corridor and I make my way to maths. Easier said than done, year 7 are making a human chain at the bottom of the stairs.
CONNOR	The one-way system has gone wrong again, it's just like one big crush. As I push through the crowd, I shut down.

Mr O'Sullivan is stood in the middle of the corridor like Gandalf, telling year 9 they shall not pass until they / 'Move to the left.'

ALL   'Move to the left.'

CONNOR   But nobody's listening.

JADE   School is dead busy but I secretly like the crowds. It's easier to disappear, like I walk past Nicole and she doesn't even notice. As I make my way to A-level law, little things start to creep in. Coz when I think about it, school is where it happened.

FLASHBACK 1

JADE   I woke up one morning and Dad had taken his motorbike and left for work without me. No warning, he'd just gone. I put my uniform on, got ready for school and thought 'Maybe he'll pick me up at home time.'

The next thing I remember is the bell ringing, grabbing my school bag and running straight into the playground. I was dead excited to ask Dad where he'd been that day. But when I got outside like no one was there, just other people's parents. I waited ages and then Mum came around the corner. She just looked at me and sobbed. In the car Mum said nothing. Literally nothing.

CONNOR   Things started to change when I was seven. My earliest memories are of Mum wearing black. In four months she lost her Mum, Dad and sister. They'd been ill since like before I was born and yeah. They all went, just like that.

For a while we coped. Mum stopped work and stayed home more, but we coped. Then things moved quite fast. Dad said he'd like gambled and lost a lot of money so we had to sell the house. Mum took me to a council house, but Dad didn't come. He got a new job and moved to Ireland.

Mum spiralled and stopped caring for herself. She was drinking and smoking and then she started talking to people who weren't there. I wanted Dad but he was far away. That meant it was up to me. I became the man of the house.

NICOLE Mum was driving me to playgroup. I was dead young, like three or four and it was a Monday. I remember coz on the Sunday night I'd made her this drawing, it was proper lame. You want me to describe it? Alright, it said 'I love you Mummy' with a little heart. Mum stuck it on the radio so whenever I'd watch her driving, I'd see my drawing.

As soon as I arrived at playgroup I was straight out the car and running to see my friends. I feel guilty about leaving because if I'd stayed, Mum would have got help sooner. Mum had a stroke outside the school gates.

JADE In the car Mum said nothing. Literally nothing. She still said nothing when we arrived at the hospital. We went straight through these massive double doors and onto the ward. I remember seeing

'Intensive Care Unit' written on the walls and wondering what it meant. I'd never heard those words before.

Mum told me Dad wasn't well, but I just thought it was a broken arm or something. We stepped into this big room and I've never seen anything like it. Everyone was hooked up to all these machines.

The whole place was noisy and crowded, but around one bed it was quiet. Mum took me over and there he was, covered in wires and tubes. All of a sudden there were loads of words being thrown between doctors and nurses, but all I wanted to ask was 'Why isn't Dad waking up?'

CONNOR   I became the man of the house because Mum needed looking after. She developed this fear of people and wouldn't go outside. She wouldn't let me leave the house. Each night I'd come downstairs and she'd be there, sat on the sofa, staring at a blank TV screen. I'd ask if she was okay, but get no reply.

Mum would just argue and worry herself into these pits and it was up to me to dig her out again. She would put this face on where her mouth was smiling, but her eyes were screaming.

NICOLE   Mum had a stroke outside the school gates. She fell out the car and started being sick. There was literally a door between us, I was like five seconds away but she was alone. Stuck between the pavement and the road.

Eventually this bloke in a massive lorry saw her. He was higher up, so he could see Mum on the floor. He stopped, picked her up, lay her sideways in the back of his lorry and drove her to hospital. When Mum arrived, the doctors said she was minutes away from dying.

JADE

'Why isn't Dad waking up?' but no one would answer. That night Will didn't have a clue what has happening. I signed to him *(she signs)* 'Dad is hurt' but it was hard to explain because Mum wasn't telling me everything. She kept on saying 'Dad came off his motorbike.' What she failed to mention was that he was in a coma, there might be brain damage and machines were the only thing keeping him alive.

Mum went to the hospital like every day while I stayed home and cared for Will. I was eight and overnight I became the parent. I always knew my brother was profoundly deaf and I always knew he had learning difficulties but I wasn't prepared for the level of care he would need. Just in terms of being told *(she signs)* 'You need to brush your teeth, you need to have a shower, you need to hang your uniform up.' Even though Will was twelve, his toileting and communication wasn't what it should have been.

One day, Mum came home, took me into the kitchen and said 'It's time Jade. The doctors are switching Dad's machines off. You need to come and say goodbye.'

CONNOR   There were no carpets in the house and it stank of rats so I started cleaning, cooking her tea, making sure she was going to bed. Literally anything to make Mum feel better again. Then we hit a point where she turned violent. Basically, she scratched me up. I kept telling myself 'It's not her fault. This person isn't my Mum.'

NICOLE   Nan moved in while Mum was away and every night she would sit me down and say 'Mum's just a bit ill, she's absolutely fine.' But later I'd overhear her on the phone being like 'I can't take Nicole to the hospital, it will only scare her.'

And I just thought no, she's my Mum I need to see her. So at breakfast I was like 'When am I seeing Mum?' On the drive to playgroup 'When am I seeing Mum?' On the drive home 'When am I seeing Mum?' At teatime 'When am I seeing Mum?' At bedtime 'When am I seeing Mum?' Eventually Nan was tucking me in and she went 'Tomorrow after school, I will take you to see your Mum.'

JADE   That car ride to say goodbye to Dad was one of those journeys where you don't want to reach your destination. The kind of journey where you sit in silence and definitely don't talk about what is going to happen.

When we got onto the ward, Dad had been moved to his own room and Mum said he'd lost ten stone. The doctors came in and one by one, they turned his machines off. I remember one of them saying 'There's nothing we can do.

The accident has left your Dad in a lot of pain and there's nothing we can do.' The lights on the machines went off, the noise stopped and I watched Dad start to suffocate.

CONNOR We had no family left, the phone was broken but even if I could use it, who would I call? I didn't want someone to take me away and I didn't want to lose my Mum. You hear so many horror stories about kids who are taken into care.

NICOLE All day at playgroup I was proper bragging that I was going to see my Mum. As soon as I got onto the ward I ran straight up to her bed, put my arms around her and was like 'It's me Mummy, I'm back.' Before she even opened her mouth, I was talking nonstop about my drawing, falling over the week before – just daft stuff.

Then there was this weird pause. Mum looked me dead in the eye, turned to Nan and went 'Who's this?'

CONNOR The worst it ever got was when Mum tried to take all her pills at once. We were in the kitchen and she went straight for the bottle. I had to stop her, I was desperate so I grabbed a knife and cut a thin slice across my neck.

JADE I was watching him struggling to breathe and I just thought 'No, he's not ready to go yet.' I didn't know what to do, so I grabbed his hand and went 'Dad, it's Jade. If you can hear me squeeze my hand.' Nothing, I tried again 'Dad it's Jade, if you can hear me squeeze

	my hand.' Nothing, I tried again 'Dad it's Jade, if you can hear me squeeze my hand.' And I felt something. It was tiny but I felt something. 'Again, I'm going to need you to do it again.' This time he grabbed my hand tight.
NICOLE	I started proper crying to Nan being like 'Mummy doesn't remember me, why doesn't Mummy remember who I am?' All I wanted was Mum to tuck me in and read me a story, but she didn't even know who I was.
JADE	I screamed at the doctors to turn the machines back on. They kept saying 'This is a normal reaction' but I was like 'Turn the machines back on, he's my Dad and I'm not letting him go.' One of the nurses finally started to do something but Dad had completely stopped breathing.
NICOLE	The only thing that went through my head was / 'Is this my life now?'
ALL	Is this my life now?
JADE	Is this it?

BUBBLE 1

Salford Young Carers Service.

MICHELLE	Would you like coffee? I didn't know what to prepare so I panicked and wrote everything down. Would you like me to read it out? I'll read it out.
PAUL	You want my life history? Jesus Christ, I need to be on a tram by quarter past.

Let's crack on. I first started working in children's homes in Greater Manchester when I was eighteen. I'd always wanted to work with disaffected young people. The kids that no one wanted. Fast forward forty-five years and I'm the Service Manager of Salford Young Carers Service.

MICHELLE At twenty-three, I started to walk a path in life I never thought I would. My eldest son was born with profound disabilities. It happened when I was in labour so there was no warning, no nothing. When his younger sister started to grow, she would ask 'Why do I have a disabled brother?' I'd tell Emma it was because she was very special, but I'd always get the same reply 'I don't want to be special, I want to be like my friends.' I remember when Emma started school, she told her teachers she was an only child.

At the time there was no service to support carers. The only support Emma got was a book from the social worker called 'Having a Disabled Sibling.'

PAUL You're looking at me blankly so I'll spell it all out. A young carer is someone aged eighteen or under who looks after a relative with a disability. In Salford, 34,000 people are caring for someone. This can range from a physical illness to mental health to drugs or alcohol addiction. 26,000 of carers in Salford are unpaid. The government doesn't offer carers any financial support if they're under eighteen.

MICHELLE	I'd never done public speaking and I wasn't political but I had no choice. Me and my daughter needed help so I started a carers group. We made presentations and met councillors to campaign for more support. We took the fight to local cabinet and won.
	In 2000, Salford Young Carers Service was founded and I've been the administrator here for over a decade. During our time, the figures we've gathered are devastating. A young carer is expected to miss forty-eight days of school a year. 68% of young carers are bullied. They are twice as likely to suffer from stress, depression, anxiety or develop a long-term illness. So yes, the odds are against them and it's getting worse. The only thing our young people seem to talk about these days is / austerity.
PAUL	Austerity is savaging young carers in Salford. The budget for Children's Services in this city has been cut by £6 million. Housing, benefit sanctions, healthcare – they're all at breaking point. We now refer children and their families to foodbanks at a rate I've never seen.
	At the Carers Service, everyone on my team should expect a caseload of around twenty. Instead everyone is on a case load of at least fifty-five. But still the message from central government is that our service should be cut, cut, / cut.
MICHELLE	Cuts are getting deeper and we can't go back to the days of no support. Me and

my daughter were unidentified and trust me, you can save a life by identifying a carer. We can't go back to having nothing.

PAUL   What happens if a carer remains unidentified? Well, there was a case in a different borough of a seventeen year old who got no support. He was the sole carer for his father who'd been in and out of hospital with an inoperable brain tumour.

One day this lad got home from school and Dad wasn't there. He went to the hospital, tried to explain the situation but the staff wouldn't say whether his Dad had been admitted. He felt like he was the only person who knew his Dad's needs and the medication he required. But because the staff didn't recognise that young people care, this lad wasn't allowed through the doors. He was sat in the corridor when they wheeled his Dad's body past.

When social services conducted their inquiry, it was found that no one, not even a doctor, teacher, neighbour, noticed something was wrong. For years this boy was carrying his father upstairs. For years there was no money coming into the house. For years this boy was left to care for his Dad alone.

As a service we do everything we can to make sure that no young person slips through the net. How can we do this when half our budget has been cut? But we're lucky to have a budget at all. There are cities across the water where young carers aren't supported at all. In Greater Manchester you have to be over twelve years old before you're eligible for support. How many children are living like this right now because we can't afford to find them?

MICHELLE   When I see our young carers come through reception, I feel for them. For thirty-three years I cared for my son. When he passed away, everything went quiet. I suppose you don't know how much you've put in until it stops. We can't just leave these young people behind. They shouldn't have to do this alone.

PAUL   The social care system is a ticking time bomb, there's only so much left to cut before we have nothing. Right, are we done here? I need to get back to work.

4

12.15pm.

NICOLE   It's lunchtime and shit is getting tribal. School has 1,400 students and we all have dinner at the exact same time. There's a queue all along the back wall and / all you can smell is curry.

JADE   All you can smell is curry and the pizza here is a crime against humanity. The dinner ladies always cook it to a million degrees and the cheese is so molten it burns your skin. / Every year the school council complain about lunch.

CONNOR   Every year the school council complain about lunch but it gets worse and more

	expensive. Since I started year 11, I've been saving leftover lunch money to buy a new computer. It's gonna cost £1,300 and I've not even scraped together ten quid. I know we live under a Tory government, but / the price of this pizza is something else.
ALL	The price of this pizza is something else.
NICOLE	Brandon isn't very smart, so I trick him into lending me a fiver for lunch. Year 7 get priority but I don't care. I push my way to the front of the queue. The dinner lady looks like Hagrid. She's wearing no gloves, no hairnet, nothing. Before I can literally say 'Please can I have' she pulls me out, gives me two behaviour points and sends me to / the back.
CONNOR	The back of the line goes crazy as Nicole is humiliated by a dinner lady. I guess that's the price you pay for breaking the rules.
JADE	On every table drama is going down like 'Mia has a moustache', 'Shane is secretly going out with Jenny' or 'Don't look now, there's that girl who dated twelve people in a week.'
	I sit and listen to people's conversations. When I started sixth form I bought a Burn Book off Amazon, so I just eat my pizza and write down what I hear. I love how much I know about everyone and no one really knows me.
CONNOR	I dump my tray, go outside and on the basketball court there's a fight between year 11 and year 12. A group of year

9s wade in and get absolutely battered. While the teachers are distracted I call Mum but she doesn't pick up.

NICOLE

I can't be arsed queuing so I go find Brandon. The staff have been asked to keep an eye on me, but it's a big school and they aren't very good at it. Me and Brandon jump the school gates and head towards the park. We think we'll get stopped but literally no one's noticed.

JADE

I'm walking to choir club when I see Chloe Grundy across the playground. Chloe's back is turned, but I can tell it's her because there's trendy rips in her blazer and her skirt is way too short. Anyway, Chloe Grundy has been chatting about me all morning. Saying stuff like 'Jade's Dad is a mong.'

She's standing in this massive group of girls. Normally I wouldn't say anything, but today I've had enough. I go over and I'm like 'Chloe, have you got a minute?' I take her to one side and I very amicably and very politely say 'I've noticed you've been making jokes about my Dad's wheelchair. If I hear you make one more I will fucking end you.'

CONNOR

I hate staying outside at lunch and being forced to socialise. The goths just hang out in the smoking shelter and talk about drugs. The plastics are caked in so much makeup you can't see their real faces and all the couples are touching each other up. Year 7s keep walking past to get a better look at the PDA.

I decide to go to the library and do homework. At the minute I'm researching a new fungus which eats bacteria and acts as a renewable energy source. I also ask myself philosophical questions.

JADE   I leave Chloe with a face that looks like a slapped arse.

CONNOR   Like is reality real?

JADE   I go and sit in choir club.

CONNOR   And if reality is real, how real am I?

JADE   But everyone there is kicking off about solos and arguing about boys and I just want to say 'Guys, can't we just sing?'

CONNOR   I close my eyes and think about the inevitable death of the universe. You know the universe started with a big bang? Well eventually it's going to expand to a point where single matter is stretched to the single atom. There won't be enough energy to contain the expansion so everything will completely compress and the world will end. Don't worry, we'll be dead by then anyway because the sun is going to blow us all up.

NICOLE   Me and Brandon are chilling on the swings when I get a call from Mum being like 'Why aren't you in school?'

When I walk back through the gates, I don't really process what happens next. All I know is that I'm starting on another kid. He's like six-foot and I just go up to him, stand on my tiptoes and smack him for no reason. The next thing I know I'm in isolation and just trashing the joint.

Tables, chairs, windows everything. I completely smash the room.

Since I started high school my behaviour's gone downhill. They're doing loads about it. I've been put onto something called a child protection plan and I'm on my thirteenth social worker but no one has actually asked me what's wrong? Why am I behaving like this? I want to tell them, but it's hard to explain.

FLASHBACK 2

NICOLE After the stroke, Mum completely lost mobility on the right side of her body. The hospital brought her home in this ambulance type thing. Once they got her in the front room she just sat in her chair, stared at the wall and wouldn't say a word.

CONNOR I was nearly eight when they took Mum away. These faceless people turned up and took her to a place called Meadowbrook. I thought it was just a boarding house or a hotel or something.

Dad realised how bad things had got and came back from Ireland. He moved me to a flat in Ashton. I'm not gonna lie, I hated him. I hated that he left, I hated he wasn't there for us. I kept reminding myself that it was his choice to do that and people make mistakes. Mum wasn't allowed visitors, so that was it. I didn't know if I would see her again.

JADE I always thought, 'Dad will either wake up or he'll die.' I wasn't prepared for all the stuff in-between. After the doctors turned the machines back on, it took three months for him to come round.

Dad still had feeding tubes and breathing support so he couldn't talk. This meant it was our job to keep his brain working. We tried everything and found music worked best. The people in the next bed were always playing Robbie Williams but Dad's favourite band was AC/DC so I blasted out 'Highway to Hell'. Yeah looking back, probably not the best song to play on repeat to a man in Intensive Care.

Every day after school I would go onto the ward and he would be that little bit better. One by one the tubes and machines disappeared until Dad was breathing on his own. He was still a long way off the seventeen stone biker he'd been before the accident, but things were moving forward. Then one afternoon the doctor came in and said 'There's no way to tell you this. The paralysis is permanent. You'll never walk again.'

NICOLE Mum wouldn't say a word, but I wasn't giving up. I needed her to talk, so I hatched a plan. Basically, for Christmas I got these fairy wings and a magic wand with a star on top. I wore them to playgroup one time and everyone was proper jealous, what can I say? Before bed I would dress up and zap her legs with my wand. Sometimes I would see her start to smile, but getting her to speak was impossible.

CONNOR	I don't know how long Mum was in Meadowbrook, time passes differently when you're a kid. But it was long enough. On the drive to pick her up, Dad said 'Mum has an illness the doctors can't fix. It's only something they can manage.' He kept saying words like bipolar and depression but I didn't understand.
JADE	When we got the news about Dad's paralysis Mum quit her job and got to work renovating the house. The whole place was turned upside down. Everything from light switches to worktops were lowered. Mum even moved a bed into the living room and turned it into Dad's bedroom, which I secretly thought was dead cool coz it was like Charlie and the Chocolate Factory.
	The day Dad was discharged me and Will pushed his wheelchair up the new ramp, through the front door and into the hallway. We'd made a huge banner painted with the words: 'Welcome home, we've missed you Dad.' The four of us had a party in the kitchen. I was wearing his blue fleece and I remember thinking 'We've fought eight months to get here and we've made it. Dad's home.'
NICOLE	Getting Mum to speak was impossible, nothing worked. Nan would check-in on us from time to time, but it was mostly just the two of us. I started to do more grown up stuff. I helped Mum put on clothes and bath time became something for her rather than me, but I didn't mind. I even did the hoovering and I hate hoovering.

At playgroup every teacher knew Mum was disabled and every teacher knew that I looked after her. All they did was give me hugs. I wanted more than that. I needed them to help.

CONNOR   When Mum came home, she was just like before. She was drinking and smoking and whispering to people who weren't there. She kept phoning the doctors, asking for something for the pain. I did a lot of research into her condition and Dad was right. This was an illness without a cure.

JADE   Our whole lives adapted to fit around Dad's wheelchair. A health worker would come in the morning and would help us get him in the shower, clean the house, do the shopping. Then they'd help with Dad's recovery. In the morning he'd learn a new word, but by the afternoon he'd forget. Some days he would learn to lift himself out of bed, but the next his joints would seize and he couldn't move.

The thing is when he first came home and I pushed his chair through the door I thought that was it – I had my Dad back. I didn't think the chair would mean anything. I wasn't prepared for how he'd changed. I wasn't prepared for how angry he'd become.

NICOLE   Mum still wasn't speaking, so I decided to try one last thing. At playgroup I was amazing at art so I made her a drawing like the one in her car. You want me to describe it? I painted in massive rainbow letters 'Just know I love you Mummy.'

When I got home I hugged her, gave her the drawing and I heard something. And then she said it again 'I love you too, you're my daughter.' For Mum to say anything was massive and she'd done it for me.

After she started speaking, it was time to focus on the bigger stuff. Mum needed to start walking again.

CONNOR

Mum would have these outbursts at Dad. She'd scream, scratch and claw with her nails until there were marks all over his face. People at work would be like 'Mate how did you get that scratch?' but he would always dodge the question. He didn't want to be a victim. And I was stuck in the middle because I was the only one Mum would listen to when she got in those moods.

JADE

After a while, I started to forget who Dad was. It felt like the Dad who took me for those rides in his truck had gone and someone else was in his place.

Mum started leaving the house whenever she could. Me and Will would just hide in our rooms. Whenever Dad went to a hospital appointment I would creep into his wardrobe and smell his old clothes and I'd never take off his blue fleece. I guess I wanted to be closer to the Dad he used to be.

CONNOR

Mum was spiralling and it was up to me to try to keep her steady. It felt like fighting an invisible battle. Her body was like healthy, but her mind was on fire.

NICOLE	It was weird to think that I only learnt to walk like three years ago and there I was teaching Mum. Slowly but surely she started to learn again, until eventually she was ready to go to the Trafford Centre.
	Mum was walking, doing proper well and it was so stupid. A piece of carpet had been folded up on the floor.
It caught her feet, she tripped and fell.
I tried picking her up but I was only four.
I was too small and she was too heavy.
This massive crowd gathered around us and I started to proper cry my eyes out.
A security guard came over and was like 'Are you okay?' and I was like 'No I'm not okay.' Mum couldn't move, her eyes were like full of pain and all I could do was watch.

5

3.29pm.

CONNOR	It's double geography. Mr Dowson has just spent forty-five minutes describing the difference between a stalagmite and a stalactite. I've known this stuff since year 7, teach me something I don't know.
ALL	I watch the clock.
JADE	Only one minute left to go.
ALL	I'm watching the clock.
NICOLE	And I'm counting down the seconds.
	10
	9

8

7

6

5

4

3

2

1

The bell rings.

ALL	I grab my bag and I'm out the door.
CONNOR	I get into the corridor.
NICOLE	The one way system has already gone to shit.
JADE	I cut through the science lab to avoid the crush.
NICOLE	Year 7 are getting ready to block the stairs.
CONNOR	Mr O'Sullivan's says / 'Move to the left.'
ALL	'Move to the left.'
CONNOR	But his heart's not really in it. I head to the lockers and grab my stuff but get caught up coz Dan is giving me trash talk about how he's gonna thrash me tonight on Call of Duty Advanced Warfare.
JADE	On my way to the bus I Facetime Will and remind him *(she signs)* 'I'm going to be late tonight.'
CONNOR	I nod along and wait for Dan to finish.

NICOLE	I'm nearly out the school gates when Gary comes out of nowhere and is like 'You're well fit, when are we going on another date?' I haven't got time, so I'm just like 'Get on my level Gary, it wasn't a date. We went to Nando's, your Mum was sat on the next table. Goodbye.'
CONNOR	I make the switch from my smart watch to my phone. I text Mum and tell her 'School's over. I'll see you soon.'

6

4.30pm.

ALL	I arrive at the surgery late, again.
JADE	It's okay because since government cut backs they're always running at least half an hour behind.
NICOLE	Mum's prescription runs out tomorrow but this was the earliest appointment I could get. Every time it's so last minute. I join the massive queue for reception.
JADE	Dad's already waiting for me. He doesn't like going in by himself. When the tannoy calls his name, the doctor won't let me in as per usual. He starts banging on about / 'doctor patient confidentiality.'
CONNOR	'Doctor patient confidentiality' is what they say every time. I'm plucking up the courage to ask why they won't let me in, but I bottle it and stay in the waiting room. Sometimes I think / there's no point me being here.

JADE	There's no point me being here if I'm not allowed to be involved in my Dad's care plan. I'm the one picking up the prescriptions, I'm the one making the appointments, I'm the one who cares for him but / no one will listen.
ALL	No one will listen.
CONNOR	The doctor's refuse to recognise me as a carer because I'm under eighteen.
NICOLE	Everyone in the surgery looks at their feet as I kick off at the receptionist. She says that because I'm not the patient, I can't pick up Mum's pills. She won't listen and keeps saying no, so I go crazy. I tell her 'My Mum's ill, I'm her daughter, give me her prescription.'
	Eventually this doctor comes out and says 'Please calm down, I'll write you a prescription, it was an honest mistake and / don't worry we'll put your name on a list.'
ALL	'Don't worry, we'll put your name on a list.'
JADE	They say that every time and it doesn't mean anything. They literally just write my name down on a blank piece of paper and that's it. I'll come back next week and it'll just be / the same.
ALL	The same excuses.
JADE	The same old reasons and / nothing ever changes.
ALL	Nothing ever changes.

FLASHBACK 3

CONNOR

One Sunday I decided to have a duvet day. It was the end of my first week of year 7, so I got in my pyjamas and sat downstairs playing video games.

JADE

Mum became distant and withdrawn. Less money was coming into the house and everything was against us. Social services were disappearing and our housing benefits had been cut. Mum finally ran out of fight. It's still no excuse for what she did.

One afternoon without any warning she packed her bags. Before Dad could even speak she was out the door. No explanation, no goodbye, nothing. Turns out Mum was having an affair.

CONNOR

As a family, we'd found our feet. Mum would still have outbursts, but we coped. Dad had completely turned his life around. Every morning before I went to school he'd make me a brew, we'd have a cuddle by ourselves and just chat. Dad would be there to pick me up from school and he became so house proud. He'd clean every room top to bottom, it was spotless. He was a different Dad to before.

Anyway, I was having this duvet day, absolutely bossing Final Fantasy 5. Then I heard this massive crash followed by like silence. I went into the hall to see what was going on and Dad was lying there. Collapsed at the bottom of the stairs.

JADE

Mum had been seeing her ex-boyfriend. When her car pulled off the drive I was shaking, I was terrified. Now it was my job to look after my brother, it was my job to look after Dad, everything was on my shoulders.

For weeks Will kept bugging me, asking what had happened until I was like *(she signs)* 'Mum has gone, she's never coming back, this is our family now so suck it up.'

CONNOR   Dad's muscles had locked and he'd fallen down the stairs. He was admitted to hospital. Doctors kept running all these tests and scans until they diagnosed him with fibromyalgia.

JADE   When Dad first had his accident, carers would come to the house for hours. Now it was fifteen minutes. In the morning someone would knock on the door, lift Dad in and out the shower, then leave.

I picked up a job before and after school to try and fill the gap that Mum left. But there were things I wasn't prepared for. Like dressing Dad, taking him to the toilet, administering injections. And all this time I could see Dad struggling. He'd lost the love of his life and he couldn't help thinking it was because of his wheelchair.

CONNOR   Fibromyalgia is a condition where you have constant pain so you get caught in this cycle of sleep deprivation, anxiety, depression and memory loss. I kept saying 'Why can't you break the cycle? Break it and you'll be fine' but he wasn't strong enough. Dad's muscles kept locking and some days he couldn't get out of bed.

I became a carer for both my parents. Two lots of appointments, two lots of pills, two lots of assessment forms. Mum and Dad are my best friends and I want to be there for them, of course I do. But it felt like the walls were closing in. Everything was caving in, I couldn't breathe.

JADE   I told my doctor my mental health was really bad. She said I could be referred to counselling but because services were so stretched it was a twelve month wait.

My life had to come second and that's fine. But I was in the first year of my A-levels, I had no friends and I was always in trouble for being late. I started skipping the bus and driving to school. But when I saw the turning, I'd just carry on driving. I didn't know where I was going. I would just carry on driving and carry on driving and carry on driving.

NICOLE   Are we talking about this now? Make sure that is definitely recording because I'm only going to say this once. Basically, Mum got a letter saying that the government was getting rid of Disability Living Allowance and everyone who was claiming benefits had to be reassessed. In the car to her appointment, Mum was proper nervous. Couldn't get her words out. Like she was well stressed because it wasn't even a trained medical professional who was going to be assessing her.

They declined her application. Mum's benefits were the only money we had coming into the house and they cut it. Her whole body was ruined by the stroke but they said she was fit for work. When Mum came home, she went straight to bed. I was like 'Mum are you okay?' and she went 'No I'm not okay.'

All night I stayed by Mum's side. In the early hours she wanted to go downstairs so I went with her. We went into the dining room. All the lights were off, so we sat in the darkness. Together. Then she went 'Look out the window Nicole.' I went over and there was nothing there. I turned around and she'd gone.

I proper pegged it into the kitchen and there was Mum, dragging a knife across her wrists. Down that way, it wasn't even sideways. Her arms don't work properly so she was using her mouth, using her teeth to push the knife into her veins.

I took the knife and rang an ambulance. Mum was sat in the kitchen bleeding and I was proper ranting like 'I'm not even in high school yet, you need to see me graduate university, get married, see your grandchildren.' The ambulance was taking ages and I was like 'Hold on, we're going to get you better.'

When the ambulance finally arrived, I wasn't allowed to get in. The paramedics said I was too young. In that moment I felt like I'd lost my Mum once and now I was losing her all over again. Watching the ambulance leave I'd like to say I was strong. But yeah.

An office.

MARY   Oh god. Okay, I'm really nervous about doing this. Are you sure you don't want my supervisor to do it? I'm just a bit worried about oversharing. You see since August, it's all started to go a bit wrong.

STEVE   Sorry it's taken us so long to meet.

MARY   Debbie? Debbie are you there?

STEVE   In a nut shell, I've worked as a part of the Carers Trust for about fifteen years.

MARY   I don't think she's coming back. Okay, if we're going to do this I'm going to need to remain anonymous. Just say that I work for a carers centre in a borough near Salford.

LISA   I was never interested in local politics growing up. To be honest, I thought Salford Council was just a bunch of old white men who didn't understand my community. Although I bloody love it, Salford is one of the poorest cities in the UK. Around 12,000 children are living in poverty. I worked as a legal secretary in East Salford and you could see it for yourself. Lower wages, more people out of work, organised crime.

            I've always had a massive gob, but in 2011 I decided to stop talking and start doing. I ran for local council and I'm now Lead Member for Children and Young People in Salford.

MARY	Well this is my first foray into the third sector. I qualified as a social worker last December and came here to do maternity cover. Then the person I was covering for never came back, so here I am: Senior Young Carers Officer.
STEVE	At the Carers Trust we work nationally with local services and councils to reach unpaid young carers. There are an estimated 700,000 young carers in the UK and since austerity began these young people are getting harder and harder to reach.
MARY	If you're here to find out what support our council gives our young carers, I think I should say 'No comment' and let Debbie answer that one.
LISA	Since 2010, austerity has cost Salford Council £180 million. Half our budget has been slashed. Now we're in a position where we can only provide people with statutory services. Anything else, we can't afford to do. I got into politics to provide services not to sit in budget meetings deciding whether we cut off our arm or our leg.
STEVE	I hate this expression, but the quality of a young carers service is a bit of a postcode lottery. Councils are bound by law to provide something. But there's no real guidelines for what its function is or how much funding it should receive. This means in times of austerity, it's up to individual councils to decide how much they value their carers service.

LISA	Yes, in 2016 we had to cut £6 million from Children's Services.
MARY	Well you've come at an interesting time because there's just been quite a lot of redundancies at our carers centre. The council came in with a red pen and started putting a cross next to people's jobs.
	We've gone from a staff body of twenty-seven to fifteen. Well actually it's less than that because more people have just left. Most mornings I look around and think 'Where have all the staff gone?' The office now is just a load of empty chairs and empty desks.
LISA	Because their parents are too ill to work, most carers depend on Disability Living Allowance. The government is in the middle of replacing this with PIPs: Personal Independence Payment. This is basically just a fancy way of saying 'We're cutting your benefits.'
	Anyone who wants to continue receiving benefits has to fill in a forty page form and go for reassessment. These are conducted by a private contractor who isn't medically trained, but is somehow expected to assess people correctly. Research has indicated nearly half of people are not awarded PIPs after their reassessment.
MARY	To be honest, I lock my feelings in a box and try not to think about what's happening. The service we provide for young carers is so strained we can't offer counselling or go into schools to identify more carers. To be honest we don't want to find any more because where would they go?

LISA	In 2012 the government decided they didn't like people appealing their benefit sanctions so they introduced a piece of legislation that removed legal aid from benefit queries. This meant that you weren't allowed a solicitor and also you had to pay up to £1,500 to submit a claim. Which is a bit of a shame considering 65% of appeals are successful. But because of this new legislation, most people can't afford to appeal.
	How is a person who is having a chaotic life with an illness expected to navigate a system and have the confidence, or money, to represent themselves? How is a young carer supposed to look after their family when they haven't got any money?
STEVE	If it's saving money the government is worried about, cutting services now only causes problems later. If a carer is unsupported they are twice as likely to need health care in later life. This means they will have to rely more on public services like the NHS. So there isn't even an economic reason why we shouldn't be supporting our young carers. If anything, there's an economic reason why we should.
MARY	Something we can offer a young person at the carers centre is support with a funding application for them to go on holiday once a year. That can be rewarding. The only thing is each case takes two months to be initially reviewed. Then there's another six week application process. Then you have to go in front of a panel. And after all that, you're lucky if you come away with fifty quid.

I suppose it's a bit of a shame when nationally young carers save the government over £30 billion a year through the unpaid caring they do and we struggle to give them fifty quid for a holiday.

There are times when I look around our empty office, I can't help but feel a bit angry. I mean how can this government feel comfortable about the fact that our whole health and social care system is propped up by children caring for their sick parents?

Oh no, have I said too much? Shit. Please don't tell Debbie.

7

5.45pm.

CONNOR	We leave the surgery and it's raining again. I'm still getting used to coming to the doctor's with Dad. Mum always fills me in but Dad's really tight lipped and won't tell me what happened in his appointment. He looks sad and starts to worry about Mum coz she's home alone. I distract him with a game of twenty questions. We stand on the corner and wait for the number 36.
JADE	Dad's got this special mobility car so he drives us home. I ask what happened at the doctor's but he struggles to remember. I look at the prescription to see what his new pills are for, but the dosage is weird and I don't understand.

NICOLE	I arrive at the pharmacy just before closing time and pick up Mum's medication. I call home and tell her tea will be late tonight and it's pasta sauce.
CONNOR	We sit at the back of the bus. We pass the Cathedral, Salford Royal and the Premier Inn. When I see them I know / I'm nearly home.
JADE	I'm nearly home, just five more minutes and I'm home. I Facetime Will and ask him to *(she signs)* 'Put the shepherd's pie in the oven' but he pulls this smug face and is like *(she signs)* 'I've binned the pie and ordered us Dominos.' I look out the window and / the rain starts to pour.
NICOLE	The rain starts to pour, it's absolutely pissing it down. I take a short cut through Blackleach Country Park Estate. There are gangs here so / I pick up the pace.
CONNOR	I pick up the pace and I don't dawdle. I take Dad's hand and we cross the road. Since they boarded up the youth centres there's always boys hanging round the corner of our street. I keep my head down as we walk past and I pick up the pace so we can get home to Mum.
ALL	At the top of my street I pass the same old things.
CONNOR	The closed down library.
JADE	The phone box with the broken phone.
NICOLE	Our neighbour's burnt out bins.
ALL	Graffiti.

JADE	And the white trainer that's been hanging on the same telephone wire for weeks.
ALL	I open the gate.
CONNOR	And I walk up the path. I stop before I open the door. I need a moment to think because I don't know what will be waiting for me when I come home.

FLASHBACK 4

JADE	I did everything I could to hide it. I didn't want anyone to know I cared for my Dad. That got harder after Mum left. Stuff started to build up. My law coursework was late, I was falling asleep in lessons. But lucky for me / teachers put it down to being a teenager.
CONNOR	Teachers put it down to being a teenager so I kept my life at home a secret. Bullies were giving me a tough time already for my glasses and stuff. I didn't want to give them any more ammunition. By now I'd been caring for my parents for eight years and / nobody knew.
ALL	Nobody knew.
JADE	Every weekend someone from choir club would be like 'Are you coming to the Trafford Centre?' or 'We're going Nando's for Helen's birthday, are you coming?' And I'd make up some lame excuse because I couldn't leave Dad on his own. I got good at lying. I made sure / I stayed hidden.
ALL	I stayed hidden.

NICOLE	Every teacher at primary school knew Mum was disabled and every teacher knew that I looked after her. Disability services had a file on me for years but they didn't do anything.
CONNOR	When I started year 11, I saw a counsellor for stress. In one session I mentioned my Mum and Dad. All of a sudden my counsellor started asking loads of questions. The next thing I knew I was filling out all these forms.
JADE	I'd been caring for my Dad for ten years before someone realised something wasn't right. My English coursework was to do an autobiography and I wrote about Dad. The next day my teacher called me into her classroom and said 'Jade, do you look after your Dad?' Ten years and she was the first person to put two and two together.
NICOLE	Nobody wanted me to be their responsibility so they just let me slip through the net. It was only when Mum hurt herself that social services got involved. Salford Council had a meeting to see whether I went through something called corporate neglect. I was in year 9 when I got a knock at the door.
JADE	A letter arrived.
CONNOR	Someone turned up at school.
NICOLE	And they said / 'Hi, I think you might be a young carer.'
ALL	'Hi, I think you might be a young carer.'

A front room.

NICOLE'S MUM Nicole has told you some stuff about me. And yeah. But this isn't about me, right? It's about her. Vulnerability. Yeah, the word is vulnerability not disability. It's like my whole life has stopped. I should be working towards a cruise in my sixties, not living like an eighty-eight-year-old biddy in a bungalow.

It sounds stupid to say out loud, but I have these dreams where I go to work. I'll wake up in the morning giddy, just thinking about the commute and what I'm going to do that day. Then I come around, realise where I am and remember. That's not me anymore.

JADE'S DAD I was in the forces before Jade and Will were born. I left because I wanted to see my kids grow. We lived in Blackpool for a time but it didn't work out, so we moved to Salford for a better life. No, that's not a sentence you hear often.

The Sunday before the accident, I'd asked Jade's Mum to marry me. To celebrate we had a party. The four us, together. Monday morning I left for work on my bike dead happy. The next thing I knew I was in a hospital bed, holding out my arm and thinking 'Whose is this?' For eight months, my life was food drip, bed bath, physio, repeat.

One morning, the doctor put a piece of bacon in front of me. I tried, but I couldn't even cut it up. I remember thinking 'How can I be a father to my kids when I can't even feed myself?'

CONNOR'S MUM   Connor was Thomas the Tank Engine mad. He had Thomas the Tank Engine bedsheets, Thomas the Tank Engine curtains – the lot. He knew the names of every single train. There were like fifty and he'd play hell if you got them mixed up. Every weekend Connor would make us get the train from Salford Crescent to Manchester Piccadilly, just to see if we could spot Thomas.

NICOLE'S MUM   I know this sounds dodgy, but it feels horrendous to be cared for.

CONNOR'S MUM   Yeah, I think my depression has made Connor grow up faster.

NICOLE'S MUM   It breaks me to have to depend on Nicole to do the things I've done naturally all my life.

CONNOR'S MUM   It's like Connor's the parent and I'm the child. He'll always ask 'Are you sure you want another fag?' or 'Do you really need another glass of wine?' And I can't help thinking 'I should be the one asking him those questions.' He's the teenager, do you know what I mean? He should be drinking in the park with his mates, not sat at home looking after his Mum and Dad.

It's hard to describe how it feels. I suppose it's like waking up some mornings and not being able to see the sun. Just darkness. I pick up a drink because it makes me feel better. I scream and hurt the people around me because at the end of the day, I don't like me.

JADE'S DAD	It was only when Jade's Mum left I realised the chair didn't make me any less of a man or any less of a Dad. Instead you just adapt. Whether it's a parents' evening, vetting a rogue boyfriend or going to a school concert, I'll be there. Even if they have to carry me in, I'll be on the front row.
	I try and tell her, but I find it hard to say. Maybe it's a bloke thing. I just want Jade to know that she's saved my life more than once. I'm getting to the point now though where I am getting older, I'm wearing out. I guess that's why I keep telling her to leave.
CONNOR'S MUM	I know I won't be able to go back to the Mum who took Connor for those train rides. Once you go through something like this, I don't think you can ever be the same. But Connor has made me realise I don't need to be that woman. I can be someone else.
	These past few months I've been leaving the house. I've started a college course and I'm going to keep pushing forward. It's little steps and sometimes I'll slip. But I know with Connor I don't have to spend my life in darkness. He helps me see the sun.
JADE'S DAD	For fifteen years my daughter has fought to make sure the accident doesn't define my life and I will fight for another fifteen to make sure it doesn't define hers.
NICOLE'S MUM	Now it's like we're under attack. The pinch of cuts and the move to PIPs is killing us. And trust me, I've tried

everything. I've gone back to work on morphine, but I can't make it through the day. I've looked at reassessment, but I can't afford it. I'm filling in forms to apply for more support, but my brain doesn't work like before. How can I fight for my family when I struggle to fill in a form?

Living like this has been like putting a complicated jigsaw back together. Without Nicole, I couldn't survive. Washing, drying, cooking, cleaning and so much more – she's there. The biggest hurdle has been getting over my pride. And yeah, Nicole has seen me at my weakest. But that hasn't stopped her.

My daughter became a carer when she was four. And there are more families with infant carers going through the same thing right now. You can't just cast us all off. We deserve more than this. That's all I need to say.

8

10.30pm.

CONNOR   The future? I've already made a plan. I want to be a scientist like Dad, but better. I'm gonna get a doctorate and start a company that constructs groundbreaking medical devices. I've learnt that not every illness has a cure, but every person deserves looking after.

JADE   I've been offered a place at Salford University to study law. I'll be the first in my family to get a degree. When I got the news, I got a tattoo. Mum always used to talk about how much she hated them, so I got a massive lioness tattoo on my shoulder blade.

It wasn't long after that I decided to wash Dad's fleece. I sniffed it and realised it was rank. Also, I don't need a blue fleece to feel close to Dad. I've got the real deal.

NICOLE   I can't live with my Mum forever. Then again, I can't leave. When I was little I had a list of all the things I wanted to do. Now I'm too old to believe in fairy tales.

CONNOR   When I was identified, I was referred to Salford Young Carers Service.

JADE   At Salford Young Carers I met people exactly like me.

NICOLE   I met people from my school who are carers. I'd walk past them every day and have no idea. Turns out anyone can be a young carer. It doesn't discriminate.

CONNOR   Life is random and bad things happen.

JADE   Your Mum could get ill. Your Dad might turn left at the junction rather than right.

NICOLE   There are hundreds of young carers in Salford. And how many more are lost in the system?

CONNOR   One in twelve kids care for someone.

NICOLE   How many more are caring alone?

JADE   But we've found each other and we're standing together.

NICOLE   Fighting together.

ALL   And building a family.

CONNOR	What would I say to young carers everywhere?
JADE	You are not on your own.
NICOLE	You are not on your own.
ALL	You are not on your own.

Beat.

CONNOR	I was in and out of hospital for about six months. I'd been getting stabbing pains which meant I couldn't move and struggled to breathe. I tried to hide the symptoms but Dad noticed and forced me to go for tests. It was the day after my seventeenth birthday when I got a call from my doctor. He asked if I could come into the surgery. I was like shit. This isn't good.

As soon as I came off the phone, Dad took me straight to the doctors. Protective instinct kicked in and he became a man possessed. We went past reception, through the waiting area and straight into the consultation room. The doctor sat me down and told me I had fibromyalgia. Dad freaked, it was the first time I'd seen him cry. Him and Grandad both suffer from fibro and I think he was having flashbacks like 'Now it's my son's turn.'

I'll never stop caring for my family, I'll never stop fighting. But some nights there comes a point where I think 'What about me? Who is going to care for me?'

Then the alarm rings. I take a breath, then it starts

An alarm rings.

Our Songs
Chosen By The Carers

First Track Of The Morning	Artist	Song
Connor	Daft Punk	One More Time
Jade	Postmodern Jukebox	Style
Nicole	Twenty One Pilots	Tear In My Heart

Music For Travelling	Artist	Song
Connor	Mitch Murder	Guile's Theme
Jade	Ed Sheeran	New Man
Nicole	Arctic Monkeys	Teddy Picker

When I Need Motivation	Artist	Song
Connor	R. Kelly	I Believe I Can Fly
Jade	Buckcherry	Crazy Bitch
Nicole	Kanye West	FML
	Arctic Monkeys	Fluorescent Adolescent

When I Rebel	Artist	Song
Connor	Beastie Boys	Fight For Your Right To Party
Jade	AC/DC	Problem Child
Nicole	Panic! At The Disco	Nicotine
	Metallica	Enter Sandman

Childhood Songs	Artist	Song
Connor	Nursery Rhyme	You Are My Sunshine
Jade	Cry Baby	Please Mr. Jailer
Nicole	John Denver	Take Me Home, Country Roads
	Christina Aguilera	Beautiful

Guilty Pleasures	Artist	Song
Connor	Dragonforce	Through The Fire and Flames
Jade	Pussycat Dolls	Don't Cha
Nicole	Miley Cyrus	Party in the U.S.A.
	Abba	Mamma Mia

Favourite Track	Artist	Song
Connor	Yoko Shimomura	Dearly Beloved (Kingdom Hearts)
Jade	Etta James	Something's Got A Hold On Me
Nicole	Twenty One Pilots	Kitchen Sink
	The Chainsmokers	Young

Songs For The End Of The World	Artist	Song
Connor	Evanescence	Bring Me To Life
Jade	DJ Casper	Cha-Cha Slide
Nicole	Panic! At The Disco	Golden Days

Songs For Our Parents	Artist	Song
Connor	Sex Pistols	God Save The Queen
Jade	AC/DC	Highway To Hell
Nicole	Tracy Chapman	Fast Car
	Luther Vandross	Dance With My Father

9 781350 306837